ALIENS AND UFOs

MARC TYLER NOBLEMAN

Chicago, Illinois

Designed by Victoria Bevan and Bigtop
Printed in China by CTPS

11 10 09
10 9 8 7 6 5 4 3 2

ISBN 13: 9781410925091

Library of Congress Cataloging-in-Publication Data

Nobleman, Marc Tyler.
  Aliens and UFOs / Marc Nobleman.
    p. cm. -- (Atomic)
  Includes bibliographical references and index.
  ISBN 1-4109-2509-9 (lib. bdg. : hc.) -- ISBN 1-
4109-2514-5 (pbk.)
  1. Unidentified flying objects--Juvenile literature.
2. Life on other planets--Juvenile literature. I.
Title. II. Series: Atomic (Series)
  TL789.2.N63 2006
  001.942--dc22

2006000229

Acknowledgments

The author and publisher are grateful to the
following for permission to reproduce copyright
material: Alamy, pp. **14–15** (Acestock Ltd), **6** (Chris
Howes/Wild Places Photography), **22–23** (Luc
Novovitch); Corbis pp. **28–29** (Darren Winter),
10-11 (Digital Art) **4–5, 8–9** (First Light); Science
Photo Library pp. **24–25** (Dr Seth Shostak),
16–17, 20–21 (Victor Habbick Visions); Topfoto
pp. **26–27**; Topfoto p. **18** (Fortean).

Cover: Cover image of flying saucers reproduced
with permission of Corbis and Tim Bird.

Every effort has been made to contact copyright
holders of any material reproduced in this book.
Any omissions will be rectified in subsequent
printings if notice is given to the publisher.

The publisher would like to thank Nancy Harris,
Diana Bentley, and Dee Reid for their assistance
in the preparation of this book.

Contents

Some words are printed in bold, **like this**. You can find out what they mean in the glossary. You can also look in the box at the bottom of the page where the word first appears.

WHAT ARE ALIENS AND UFOS?

Our solar system has nine planets. As far as we know, living things exist on only one of them: Earth. There are many planets outside our solar system. We do not know if any of them have life. However, some people believe that we are not alone in the universe.

Visitors from another planet?

An alien is a living being from a planet other than Earth. That could mean a wide range of things, from a 10-foot- (3-meter-) tall creature to a **microscopic virus**.

UFO stands for "unidentified flying object." Many people think aliens travel through space in UFOs.

This is our solar system. Do you think there could be life in another solar system?

Some people think aliens have visited Earth in spaceships such as this one.

microscopic	something so tiny that you need a microscope to see it
solar system	group of planets that circle around a sun
universe	Earth, all the planets, stars, atmosphere, and space
virus	tiny form of life that can make people sick

Some people believe that cave paintings show aliens. This cave art is thousands of years old.

UFOS IN HISTORY

People began to use the term "UFO" in the 1950s, but people said they saw UFOs long before that.

Aliens in the ancient world

Some **cave paintings** in France and Australia include flying vehicles that look like UFOs. Figures in the paintings wear what look like helmets.

In ancient times people reported strange flying shields in places such as Rome and India. Sometimes the shields were shining. Others seemed to be burning.

What do you think?

Archaeologists around the world have found relics that show scenes with bright, round objects floating in the sky. Were these drawings of UFOs?

archaeologist	person who studies ancient people
cave painting	art that an ancient human painted on a cave wall
relic	object from the past

WHAT ALIENS LOOK LIKE

Thousands of people claim they have seen aliens. Many of them describe aliens as gray, short, and thin. Others claim that aliens look like reptiles.

Alien bodies

Some people think aliens are probably close to our size, or at least smaller than an elephant. If they were very large, they might be too heavy to walk around easily.

On Earth all things that live in the light have eyes. Therefore, some people assume that aliens living in light would have eyes, too. However, their eyes might not be above their noses like ours are!

Alien mysteries

Aliens may come from more than one planet. They may look different from humans and from one another.

Aliens are often described as having large heads, large black eyes, and no hair.

UFOs such as this have been reported, and even photographed, traveling very fast. Many are discs between 30 and 100 feet (9.1 and 30.5 meters) wide.

What UFOs Look Like

Witnesses often describe UFOs as silver, dish-shaped objects. For this reason, UFOs used to be called flying saucers.

Lights in the sky

Sometimes people claim to see odd lights before a UFO sighting. The flying objects are said to fly faster than any human-made aircraft. They can move against the wind or disappear quickly.

Mistakes and mysteries

About 90 percent of reported UFO sightings turn out to be something else. People have mistaken **weather balloons**, kites, planes, or even the planet Venus for UFOs. However, that still means 10 percent are a mystery.

disc	round and flat shape
weather balloon	balloon that carries equipment to measure weather conditions
witness	person who sees an event happen

UFO AND ALIEN SIGHTINGS

All kinds of people claim to have seen aliens and UFOs, usually at night. Some people did not believe in aliens until their experiences.

Types of close encounter

Astronomer J. Allen Hynek created a system to describe UFO sightings. He suggested three types of "close **encounter**". In each case, the **witness** must be no more than 500 feet (152 meters) away.

> 1. A close encounter of the first kind is seeing a UFO.

astronomer	person who studies space
encounter	meeting

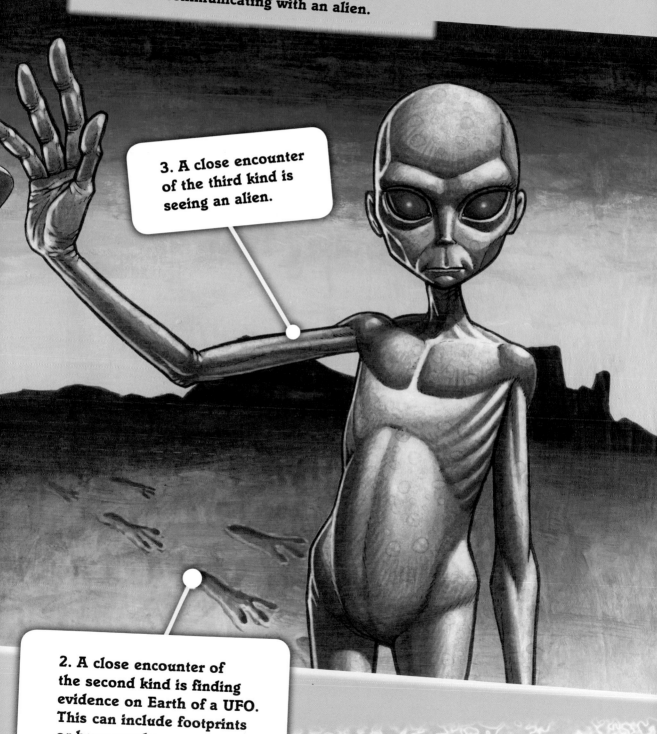

Two other categories of close encounter are sometimes mentioned. The fourth kind is going on board a UFO. The fifth kind is communicating with an alien.

3. A close encounter of the third kind is seeing an alien.

2. A close encounter of the second kind is finding evidence on Earth of a UFO. This can include footprints or burn marks.

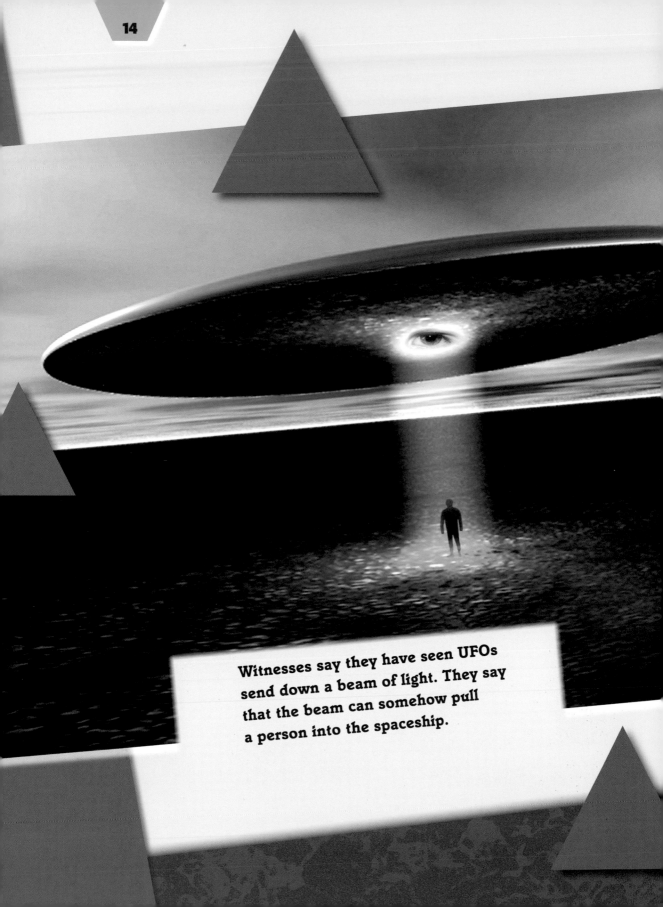

Witnesses say they have seen UFOs send down a beam of light. They say that the beam can somehow pull a person into the spaceship.

ABDUCTION

The fourth kind of close encounter can include **abduction**. This is when aliens take people into a UFO, whether or not they want to go.

After an abduction

After people who believe they were abducted return, some say the aliens did scientific tests on them. Some say the aliens used **telepathy**, which is talking with thoughts, not speech. Others do not remember what happened.

What do you think?

Some people may not tell others they believe they were abducted. They worry that no one will believe them. What would you do?

abduction	taking a person somewhere against his or her wishes
telepathy	ability to talk with thoughts instead of speech

MEN IN BLACK

A UFO sighting does not always end when the UFO leaves.

Strange visitors

Sometimes **witnesses** have reported bizarre visitors coming to their homes soon after a sighting. The visitors may pretend to work for the government. These "Men in Black" have bulging eyes. Their voices sound electronic.

Scary warnings

Men in Black tell witnesses that they should not have seen what they did. They warn them to keep it secret. Unlike the characters in the movie *Men in Black* (1997), these Men in Black are not funny and probably not human.

Alien fact

"Men in Black" are often described as driving old black cars and dressing in dark suits.

Men in Black may be
aliens themselves.

Roswell Daily Record

ROSWELL, NEW MEXICO, WEDNESDAY, JULY 9 1947

Leased Wire
Associated Press

RECORD PHONES
Business Office 2288
News Department
2287

VOL. 47, NUMBER 100 ESTABLISHED 1888

Gen. Ramey Empties Roswell Saucer

Lewis Pushes Advantage in New Contract

Southern Mines Only Hold-outs In New Contract

Sheriff Wilcox Takes Leading Role in Excitement Over Report 'Saucer' Found

Arrest 2,000 In Athens in Commie Plot

Revolution Was Set to Be Pulled Off Thursday

Send First Roswell Wire Photos from Record Office

Romania Rejects Bid to Take Part In Economic Meet

Ramey Says Excitement Is Not Justified

General Ramey Says Disk Is Weather Balloon

The object seen in Roswell may have been a **weather balloon** or a **UFO**. Newspaper stories about the event stirred up excitement.

UFO CRASH?

In July 1947 people spotted aircraft resembling UFOs over New Mexico. Days later, something crashed near the town of Roswell, New Mexico (see map).

A weird discovery

A **rancher** found shiny objects in the desert, which were unlike anything he had seen before. Some pieces looked like metal but could not be cut, creased, or burned. Weird letters and numbers were on other pieces. The rancher told the police, who told the **military**.

What do you think?

Soldiers took everything from the site in Roswell immediately. They told witnesses never to talk about it. Why do you think they wanted to keep it secret?

military	the army
rancher	person who works on a farm that raises cattle

CROP CIRCLES

Crop circles are large designs found in fields. They are created when crops are bent into patterns. Thousands have appeared around the world.

Causes of crop circles

Most crop circles appear overnight. In some the plants are crushed, while in others the plants have been gently bent over. Some crop circles are not circles at all. They are complex shapes.

Many people think that humans make crop circles. Some think they are natural, while others believe the heat or **landing gear** from UFOs causes some crop circles.

What do you think?

Sometimes people admit they made a hoax crop circle. But are they all hoaxes?

Many people think aliens make some crop circles.

hoax
fake

landing gear
part of an airplane or spaceship that helps it land

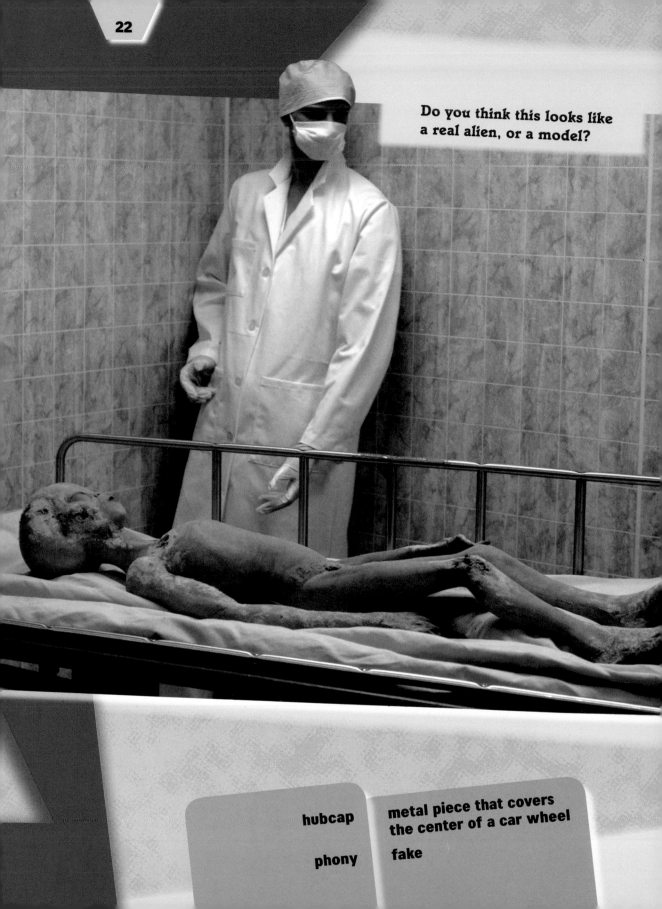

Do you think this looks like a real alien, or a model?

hubcap — metal piece that covers the center of a car wheel

phony — fake

COSMIC HOAXES

Some people make up UFO or alien stories to fool others.

Amazing fakes

Crop circles are often **hoaxes**. A farmer might find one in his field, and he thinks it may have been made by aliens. Later, other humans admit that they did it.

Some people have thrown a **hubcap** in the air and photographed it. Then, they say they photographed a UFO.

Dead alien on film

In the 1990s a TV show aired a video of doctors studying the dead body of an alien. Some people were amazed. However, the TV company later admitted it was **phony**.

What do you think?

Why have people tried to trick others by making hoax alien films or photos?

SEARCHING FOR ALIEN LIFE

People look for aliens in many ways. Some camp out by fields. They hope to see a crop circle being formed.

Searching for aliens with science

Scientists use more technical methods. **NASA** has sent robots to Mars to look for signs of life. If a robot finds water below the surface, Mars may be home to **microscopic** living things that need water to survive.

The Search for **Extraterrestrial** Intelligence Institute (SETI) has been looking for aliens for years. This organization believes aliens might be sending radio signals into space.

What do you think?

NASA and SETI keep searching for alien life. Do you think they are wasting their time?

SETI uses satellite dishes to listen for alien signals.

extraterrestrial	living thing that is not from Earth
NASA	(National Aeronautics and Space Administration) U.S. government organization that studies space

In the movie E.T. (1982), an alien is stranded on Earth and makes friends with a boy.

Aliens and UFOs in Popular Culture

Actually, many aliens are already on Earth—in books, movies, TV shows, and comic books.

Alien stories

The War of the Worlds by H. G. Wells was published in 1898. This book is about a Martian invasion of Earth. In 1938 a radio broadcast of this story terrified listeners, bcause many people thought it was a real news event.

Aliens on screen

In the movie *Independence Day* (1996), aliens invade Earth, but in *E.T.* the alien is gentle and curious.

Friendly alien characters have appeared on TV shows including *Star Trek*.

Alien mysteries

Even Superman is an alien. He is from the planet Krypton.

ARE ALIENS AND UFOS REAL?

Some people think aliens and UFOs are not real. Others say they are—even people who have never seen one. However, no one is certain.

We need proof

Stories, photographs, and crop circles are not enough **proof** for scientists. The only kind of proof of aliens and UFOs that scientists will accept is physical proof. This means they must meet an alien or find a UFO.

Aliens may be out there, but that does not mean they can travel or even send signals to Earth. Maybe one day we will be able to travel to *their* planet. What do you think?

Perhaps we will never know the truth about aliens and UFOs.

proof   facts

Glossary

abduction taking a person somewhere against his or her wishes

archaeologist person who studies ancient people

astronomer person who studies outer space

cave painting art that an ancient human painted on a cave wall

disc round and flat shape

encounter meeting

extraterrestrial living thing that is not from Earth

hoax fake

hubcap metal piece that covers the center of a car wheel

landing gear part of an airplane or spaceship that helps it land

microscopic something so tiny it cannot be seen without a microscope

military the army

NASA (National Aeronautics and Space Administration) U.S. government organization that studies space

phony fake

proof facts

rancher person who works on a farm that raises cattle

relic object from the past

solar system group of planets that circle around a sun

telepathy ability to talk with thoughts instead of speech

universe Earth, all the planets, stars, atmosphere, and space

virus tiny form of life that can make people sick

weather balloon balloon that carries equipment to measure weather conditions

witness person who sees an event happen

Want to Know More?

Books

* Krull, Kathleen. *What Really Happened in Roswell?: Just the Facts (Plus the Rumors)* New York: Harper Collins, 2003.

* Oxlade, Chris. *The Mystery of Crop Circles (Can Science Solve . . ?)* Chicago: Heinemann Library, 2006.

* *Royston, Angela. Alien Neighbors? (Fusion: Physical processes and materials)* Chicago: Raintree, 2006.

Websites

* www.aliensmonstrous.com
  Find out about different types of aliens.

* www.ufoevidence.org
  Click on "photographs" and decide if you believe UFOs really exist!

* www.ufosabout.com
  Search the site for information on crop circles, aliens, and UFOs.

If you liked this Atomic book, why don't you try these...?

Index